The Lost Village of BUCKHAV

by

Eric Eunson

Children's Corner. Buckhaven

Oldtown. Buckhaven.

M. 113

INTRODUCTION

The most popularly quoted account of the foundation of the village of Buckhaven is taken from a letter written by the Reverend Harry Spens, the ex-minister of Wemyss parish, to his successor George Gib in 1778. Spens states that according to local tradition the original inhabitants were the crew of a Dutch vessel, wrecked on the shore near the site of the village. It is said that they approached the Laird of Wemyss for permission to settle there and that this was duly granted. It has been suggested that they were refugees from religious persecution, but equally they could have been merchants or fishermen. All this is supposed to have taken place during the second half of the 16th century. It is, however, a verbal tradition that was itself two hundred years old when written down by Spens, so its accuracy is open to doubt.

An authentic mention of the village appears in 1516. In this year the fishermen of Easter Wemyss and Buckhaven were called upon to support their landlord, the Laird of Wemyss, in a dispute over his contribution to the minister's stipend.

There are two theories how Buckhaven came by its name. One suggests it is derived from "Baile Euan" meaning Ewan's town. The other, more probable, solution is that it is a hybrid of the Gaelic "Buc or Beuc", to roar, and the Norse word "Haven" meaning a harbour. The village had no man-made harbour until the 19th century and for centuries the only protection offered to its fishing boats was provided in the shelter of two skerries of rocks jutting into the sea. These were known as the East and West Hynes. The name "roaring harbour" is said to be taken from the sound of the waves crashing upon these rocks.

Whenever it was founded, the principal industry of the village would always appear to have been fishing. The absence of a proper harbour prevented it becoming a centre of trade. When Daniel Defoe visited Buckhaven in 1700 he described a place entirely engaged in fishing. He also called it "a miserable row of cottages", but added "yet there is scarce a poor man in it". The village of Defoe's time had grown between the two "Hynes", straggling along the shore, and branching into its only two streets – East and West High Street. Between these the other buildings were randomly scattered following the contours of the hill and intersected with narrow, winding lanes.

In 1700 most of the fish caught at Buckhaven was sold in Edinburgh, but by 1750 the Edinburgh buyers preferred the catches of the East Neuk fleets. As they fished further offshore the fish tended to be larger than those caught by the inshore boats of Buckhaven. By now the village had changed to supplying a substantial landward area of Fife with fresh fish. The catches were loaded into wicker panniers on the backs of horses and "cadged" in farming areas and towns. This provided employment for a large proportion of the village population, but had almost died away by 1800. Around this date many of the fishermen became handloom weavers, while others turned to the comparative security of farm labouring.

In 1750 it was not unusual for as many as 25,000 fish to be landed at Buckhaven in a single day, but forty years later the whole fishing economy of the Firth of Forth was on the verge of collapse as fish became very scarce. In neighbouring places such as Leven and Largo the industry was temporarily abandoned altogether, but the Buckhaven fishers persevered. Sixty of its hundred and forty families continued to try and make a living from the sea and it is recorded that they were at least partly compensated for the shortage of fish by much higher prices.

From 1794 onwards the fortunes of the fishermen revived. Huge shoals of herring appeared again in the forth. At Burntisland over 900 boats from both sides of the Forth congregated annually for the winter herring fishing, whilst the summer herring fishing centred on Dunbar.

In 1805 fish curers in Wick perfected a means of preserving herring for a long time by packing the gutted fish in barrels filled with coarse salt and brine. Curing fish in this way meant that they could be exported to wider European markets. This development was to lead to the great herring industry of Scotland that was to last for nearly a century and a half. Around 1810 Buckhaven boats were among a fleet of over a thousand vessels that came from every port north of Berwick to congregate on the rich grounds of the Caithness coast. Herring quickly replaced white fish as the principal catch of Buckhaven fishermen and the seasonal journeys to distant ports became longer and more frequent.

In 1831 Buckhaven had 198 boat, the second largest fleet in Scotland. But it still had no proper harbour and all these boats had to be beached when not in use. Larger boats were needed for the profitable offshore voyages and the village was in danger of being overtaken by other ports with superior harbours. The community approached the Fishery Officer with a petition for the construction of a harbour. This was approved and work began in 1837, with much of the cost of construction being raised by the fishermen themselves.

The heyday of Buckhaven's fisheries seems to have been in the 1850s, when 168 boats provided employment for more than 500 men and boys. For a few years Buckhaven became a curing station and attracted English fish buyers. But the prosperity was short lived, the herring migration changed, and they deserted the Forth. Buckhaven boats continued to travel to such places as Caithness, Aberdeenshire, Stornoway, and the English ports of North Shields and Yarmouth, while their home port had lost much of its importance and reputation. The decline was partly blamed on local collieries and partly on the effects of trawling on the inshore grounds. This latter problem may have been a local disaster partly caused by the Buckhaven fishermen themselves. In the 1870s, a method of fishing called the "Beam Trawl" was used by a number of local boats, although it was not popular elsewhere. An ordinary trawl net takes the form of a tapered bag, which is pulled through the sea some distance above the seabed. The "Beam Trawl" was so-called because the mouth of the net was kept open by a heavy, three-sided structure of wooden beams with a rope along the bottom edge. The weight of the beams meant that this rope scoured across the sea bed, resulting in damage to spawning and shellfish grounds. All trawling in the Firth of Forth was banned by the imposing of a three mile offshore limit in the 1880s, but by then considerable damage had been done to many of the local grounds.

Although it could be highly profitable in a good season, the fortunes of fishing were uncertain. In 1864 Messrs. Bowman & Co. bought the lease of the Muiredge Colliery about half a mile from Buckhaven. The effect on the community was dramatic as more and more young men were tempted to leave the fishing for the prospect of steady work in the mine. Muiredge proved so successful, that in the early 1870's the firm sank three more local collieries.

In 1878 the harbour held a fleet of 93 boats. Ten years later this number had fallen to 74. Another decade saw this plummet to only 40. In 1894 the last boatbuilder in the village gave up his craft and turned his attention to making pit props. In 1904-5 Buckhaven sent 35 boats to North Shields, but catches were poor. Of the twenty boats still using the harbour in 1908, only five remained by the start of the First World War.

The expansion of the collieries from the 1870s onwards, brought an influx of immigrant workers to the village to fill the new jobs. Between 1871 and 1901 Buckhaven's population grew from 2187 to 4522. The first wave of incomers were mostly former shale miners from West Lothian. They were soon joined by colliers from declining coalfields in Ayrshire and North Lanarkshire. New houses were built at the "Braehead" area of the village to house these workers.

4

In 1905 the Denbeath Colliery was acquired by the Wemyss Coal Company, renamed the Wellesley Colliery, and greatly improved and enlarged. An early consequence of this was that the hamlet of Links of Denbeath, the easternmost extension of Buckhaven, was in the way of the rapidly growing spoil heap of the pit. The Links was evacuated and, along with the old coast road to Leven, was gradually buried in colliery waste. Despite reassurances from the mine owners that Buckhaven would not share the same fate, the vast bing continued to grow. Eventually the sloppy and thoughtless practice of dumping the waste into the sea began. The choking of the old village had begun in earnest.

In 1920 nearly 200 new council houses were built on and around Wellesley Road. These had all the modern conveniences and sanitation that were often lacking in the old fisher cottages. Naturally, many families left their old homes on the shore in favour of these comfortable new houses.

Over the next thirty years the prehistoric muck from the Wellesley continued to bury the foreshore of the village. By the early thirties the harbour had become so clogged by the drifting slag that the lifeboat house had to be closed.

The fishing industry here was gone forever and more and more of the old houses were left to fall derelict. But, despite this, many families still clung proudly to their traditional family homes. The choice, however, was soon to be lifted from them. The visions of post war planners had no room for a refurbished antique village.

Although Buckhaven was unique in character, the random scattering of its layout made it unlike any other fishing villages in the county, it was run-down and lacking many of the basic essentials of modern living. In 1960 the condemning of the whole of the old fishing village began. Many local people protested, but the bulldozers moved in regardless. Within ten years hardly a trace of the once thriving community remained. The rubble from the houses was dumped on what remained of the foreshore and harbour, obliterating any features that the bing had spared. Ironically, at the same time as this wanton vandalism was taking place, the National Trust were engaged in restoring similar houses to those being destroyed in other parts of Fife.

The replacements for the old houses added insult to injury. A development of brooding, characterless concrete rectangles in a style that was already controversial in other places. These flat-roofed buildings, unsuited to the wet and exposed climate of the area, are fraught with problems of damp and heating. Like so many contemporary developments, they may well be destined to an uncertain future.

Did "Old Buckhyne" have to go? Many buildings were certainly completely derelict by the 1960s, but many others were inhabited right up to their demolition. Had part of the village been spared it could have been an asset to local tourism. As it is, Buckhaven today is an unhappy place, a town of shut pits, abandoned shops and unpopular housing. The looming bing of the Wellesley has been partly levelled and the site used to build oil rigs. A great rubble wall fringes the sad village, a hundred yards beyond the old foreshore. The sea that breaks on it is still slate grey with colliery waste.

Acknowledgements: I would like to thank Campbell McCutcheon for permission to use the photograph on the inside front cover and page 31, and W.A.C. Smith for the use of the photograph on page 6.

A branch line from Thornton Junction to Buckhaven was opened on August 1st 1881. It was built and run by the Wemyss family. In 1887 the track was extended to Methil to serve the new dock there. Two years later the Wemyss family sold both the Wemyss and Buckhaven Railway and Methil dock to the North British Railway. The N.B.R. was absorbed into the London and North Eastern Railway in 1923, and they continued to operate the line until nationalisation. Declining traffic and coastal erosion led to the ceasing of regular passenger services in 1955 and the eventual closure of the line in 1966. This photograph dates from 1958 and shows a rare passenger train to Methil, a football special from Glasgow, Queen Street. In the background are the ruins of the old Buckhaven Gas Works. From 1846 to 1923 it supplied gas to Buckhaven, East Wemyss, Methil and Rosie.

Beside the Seaside. Buckhaven

Concert parties were a popular attraction at Buckhaven from the turn of the century until the start of World War Two. In the 1930s seats cost ninepence and sixpence, depending on whether you opted for a deckchair or a wooden form. If you sat on the Brae outside the enclosure then it cost only a penny. The sender of this 1924 postcard to Burton on Trent in Staffordshire says of Buckhaven "the people are all right, but can't tell what they say".

4939. At the Seashore, Buckhaven.

Buckhaven became a popular place for a seaside holiday during the interwar years. Families from the industrial towns and cities of Central Scotland came here in droves during their respective, unpaid, "fair fortnights". After the war, the pit bing had begun to encroach on the golden West Sands, seen here in 1930, turning them black. Buckhaven could no longer offer the attraction of neighbouring resorts like Leven and Largo and the holidaymakers deserted it.

Buckhaven Sands

4938

Improvements to Buckhaven beach were carried out in 1926, partly to attract more visitors and partly to relieve local unemployment. These included the construction of a bandstand (right), a bathing pool, and a promenade linking this with the Harbourhead. The old cottages shown on page 7 were converted into changing rooms for bathers. Today, much of the beach and sea in this 1930 picture have been buried under rubble from the old village, which has been grassed over replacing this scene with a big windswept lawn.

BATHING POOL, BUCKHAVEN.   207559.J.V.

The bathing pool was nicknamed rather scathingly by many locals as "Provost Mackay's Dream Pond". For its first year the pool was filled by the tide, but it kept filling up with sand so a wall was built around it and a pump installed to regulate the water level. The provost's dream was short lived, though, and the pool was closed entirely in 1939 as it was considered unsanitary. It is shown here in 1929.

Harbour, Buckhaven

The fishermen of Buckhaven formed themselves into a society to raise money for the construction of a harbour in 1822. By the time they approached the Fishery Board in 1835 they had raised more than £1200. The Board added a further £3000 to this, and work on the East breakwater was completed three years later. The West Pier was added in 1840, and the whole harbour further enlarged in 1853, with the fishermen again contributing substantially to the cost of the work. This 1905 postcard shows 31 boats of Buckhaven's herring fleet.

The Harbour. Buckhaven.

M. 113

The East Pier and Lighthouse in the early 1930s. In January 1939 a great storm swept more than thirty yards of this stone pier into the sea. Since the harbour was now home to only a handful of boats it was simply left to the elements. Finally, the lighthouse collapsed in 1942. Little of the harbour wall remains today, and the basin was infilled with rubble from the redevelopment of the village and the demolition of the Wellesley Colliery. Among the refuse that lies on the strip of black sand at the mouth of the forgotten harbour are sea-worn bricks bearing the names of the colliers Bowman and Wemyss.

THE HARBOUR. BUCKHAVEN

At the start of the 19th century most Buckhaven boats measured less than twenty feet in length, but as longer voyages became necessary this increased to between 34 and 39 feet. All Scottish boats were undecked until 1855, since fishermen claimed that open boats were easier to work from, but safety saw the universal adoption of decks by around 1880. By 1870 Buckhaven had two boatbuilders, Mungo Baird and David Brown, and they built most of the local vessels. Before this most Buckhaven boats were built at Leith. The craft in this 1925 illustration, and on the facing page, are of a type known as ":Baldies", after the Italian patriot, Garibaldi. These boats were popular throughout the east of Scotland from around 1880. Usually measuring less than 20 feet along the keel, these boats made up Buckhaven's inshore fleet.

Home from the Herring Fishing, Buckhaven

Left: For long voyages in pursuit of herring the most popular boats along the Firth of Forth were "Fifies". Similar in design to the smaller "Baldies", they were distinguished by their poker-straight stem and stern (front and rear). This is the 52 foot "Gratti": KY565 built by David Brown at his West Sands boatyard in 1894. She was one of the last two boats built in the village. Although by 1900 steam had largely superceded sail as the most popular way of powering fishing boats, Buckhaven fishermen did not favour the new vessels. Instead many of the larger boats like the "Gratti" were fitted with Kelvin motors. These were started using petrol, then run on cheaper paraffin once they had warmed up.

Right: A model "Baldie" is demonstrated by "Telford" Thomson to young Alex Warrender. Until the immigration of the late 19th century there were only a handful of surnames in the village and Deas, Foster, Logie, Robertson, Walker, Warrender and scores of Thomson's accounted for ninety percent of the population. In order to make identification easier nicknames, known as "slug" or "tee" names, were used. These were often taken from the name of a fishing boat or the location of a fisherman's home.

A Chip of the Old Block

A 1903 picture entitled "Sharing the Fish". When the small inshore boats landed their catches, it was customary to divide the fish equally among the crew. The fish were then sold in the village and neighbouring towns by the women of the fishermen's families. Buckhaven fishwives wore a distinctive dark blue costume. In the centre of the photograph are two wicker baskets, one inside the other. When full the women carried the larger of these on their backs, with the smaller rounded one resting on top of this behind their heads. These baskets were known as back and head creels.

LAUNCH OF LIFE-BOAT, BUCKHAVEN

The lifeboat station at Buckhaven was opened in 1900. The rescue vessel was named "Isabella" after Mrs. Isabella Haxton of Kirkcaldy who bequeathed the money used to build her. She had a crew of twelve and was launched nineteen times in emergencies. Lifeboat demonstrations were popular with locals and tourists alike as can be seen from the crowds gathered to watch this pre WW1 display. The clogging of the harbour caused her to be withdrawn from service in 1932. She later became a pleasure cruiser at North Queensferry, and ended her days running between Gourock and Greenock. The ruined lifeboat house was finally pulled down along with the rest of the Harbourhead in 1963.

Buckhaven and Methil Fire Brigade's new engine being tested on the East Pier in 1909. From 1909–1939 the fire station was located in Alison Street, behind the municipal buildings, before being moved to its present site at Crossroads, Methil. This engine, a Merryweather "Fire King", was in service until 1931.

This little row of cottages which stood to the rear of the Harbour Head were known grandly as the West End, a statement of geographical fact rather than implied prestige! The photograph dates from 1904.

West High Street, Buckhaven

This 1907 view was taken from a similar vantage point to the previous picture but looking east. Although the upper part of West High Street escaped the bulldozers Foster's haberdashery shop and the hairpin bend are now but a memory.

BAITING THE LINE   BUCKHAVEN

A 1903 photograph of the Robertson family. This old fashioned method of fishing was known as the small (or sma') line, and it involved baiting some eight hundred individual hooks on a single line with mussels. The wife is shelling the mussels while her husband attaches them to the hooks. Behind her is a hand barrow used to transport the fishing gear to and from the boats.

BAITING THE LINE.

Left: A 1904 photograph of Margaret Thomson and her father "Peter O' the Hyne". The women in a fishing family performed many of the ancillary tasks of the industry. They mended nets, collected bait, carried the fish to market and usually baited the lines. They also knitted most of the sea clothes used by the fishermen, such as this "gansey" worn by Peter. The patterns of these were distinct to an individual port and were handed down from generation to generation.

Right: John Warrender "redding" or disentangling the line, a task which had to be performed after every fishing. As well as removing tangles and checking for damage, any old bait had to be taken off to prevent it rotting. The wooden box to his left was known as a scull. At the curved end was an aperture, through which the line was fed during fishing. When the whole line had been cast, the boat returned to where it had begun, and the line was hauled. Sma' lining was used inshore, mainly to catch haddock. Although labour intensive, this method of fishing was still used in East Neuk ports until the 1930s.

Buckhaven, Fisherman Redding the Line

Left" For offshore herring fishing huge cotton drift nets were used. This cotton; the hemp ropes used at sea; and the sails of boats were all prevented from rotting by "barking". This involved immersing them in a boiling solution of "cutch" (a derivative of oak bark). This gave the nets a deep chestnut brown hue.

Right: Mary Thomson – "Concord" girding or mending the nets. Despite treatment, the cotton nets still needed frequent repair after catching on underwater obstacles or damage from the fishermen's enemies – dogfish and conger eels – which could virtually destroy a net. White nets like this one were only used in the Firth of Forth during the winter fishing.

GIRDING THE NET.

Left: Conditions in the fishing quarter of Buckhaven were primitive at the turn of the century. Most families still relied on communal wells for fresh water. In spite of this the fisherfolk regarded themselves as a cut above the dusty miners and they took great pride in the cleanliness of their homes and their persons.

Right: John "Sovereign" Deas in a 1903 study entitled "World's End". The world of the Buckhaven fisherfolk was indeed coming to an end. The Scottish fishing industry, of which the village had once played a great part had many good years to run but Buckhaven was no longer involved. The young men were drawn to the collieries, leaving an ageing community of fishermen that would eventually die out altogether. In 1930 only 28 fishermen remained in the village.

The harbour ruins are the only landmark remaining to locate this view. Had a 1905 scheme gone ahead, the foreshore of Buckhaven would have been destroyed even earlier than it was. Randolph Wemyss, landowner and industrialist, approached parliament to build a huge dock at Buckhaven. He claimed the dock was necessary in order to relieve congestion at neighbouring Methil. Wemyss had in fact strong motives of his own for the project. He had sold Methil dock to the North British Railway in 1889 and become a director of the company. He resigned after a quarrel with his fellow directors in 1899 and now, with the expansion of his own collieries, was annually paying the N.B.R. handling charges on a million tons of his coal from Methil. Had the plan gone ahead, Buckhaven would have been flanked from the harbour to the Hyne Head by docks and marshalling yards. Unfortunately for Wemyss, while parliament conceded a traffic problem existed at Methil, they decided the best solution was to allow the N.B.R. to expand their docks at Methil.

24

The Fore Doors, Buckhaven

This 1905 picture was taken just to the east of the one on the facing page. Outside stairs, or fore-stairs, are a classic feature of fishermen's houses in the east of Fife. Comparison of contemporary photographs confirms that Buckhaven had more of these than any other town or village in the county. Under many was a niche, the depth of the steps and the height of a door. These were used to shelter the fishermen from the elements while preparing their gear.

The Shore, Buckhaven.

The shore in 1903, looking east along the Fore Doors, and West Shore Street, to Hyne Head. The unique building with the arched windows in the foreground housed the premises of William Dawson, grocer and wine merchant. The poles on the beach were known as "galluses" and were used for drying the nets.

Buckhaven — West Shore Street

not such a nice shore as Largo eh Daisy.

A 1904 picture postcard from a photograph by one of Buckhaven's many James Thomson's. This one had a stationer's shop and studio in Church Street and his postcards form an invaluable part of the record of old Buckhaven. Daisy, the sender of the card remarks that the shore is not as nice as the one at Largo. In fact at the time the two were very similar, with sand running down to beds of shingle and waterworn boulders. If Daisy could only see it now!

The Broken Brae, Buckhaven

The houses at Broken Brae took their name from the outcrop of sandstone on the right of this 1905 photo. Today it is the only feature still recognisable, lying in between two brooding blocks of flats at Mid Shore. The old houses of the village fell into two basic types, both of which are shown here. The two on the left were built of sandstone. This was usually protected from the corrosive effects of the elements with a plaster coating which was painted. The house on the right was built of much harder black whinstone which did not need to be protected. In whinstone houses, sandstone was invariably used for window and door surrounds and outside stairs.

28

OLD BUCKHAVEN

Broken Brae is the second group of houses from the left in this late 1930s picture. The persistent dumping of outpourings from the Wellesley had accumulated to such and extent that they buried the foreshore to a depth of fifteen feet! Only the top of the sea wall in the preceding photograph is visible and a road has been driven across the debris in front of it. But, in spite of their dismal outlook, the houses still look spruce and freshly painted.

Death of a village – 1957. In less than twenty years Buckhaven went steadily downhill, with many old houses abandoned. Their decay was helped along by the iniquitous law that used to exist, which meant rates were not payable on a building if the roof was removed. Patches of seaweed in the foreground of this picture mark the new tide line of the village.

A photograph of the same scene today. I will leave the readers to form their own opinions about whether or not the view has improved. In a recent survey more than half of the tenants of Lower Buckhaven had applied for a transfer to other council houses. The most common complaints were of dampness, vandalism, lack of maintenance and poor lighting around buildings.

These houses stood just to the west of the Hyne Head. All the fishermen's houses in the old town had roofs made of red pantiles. These concave clay tiles originally arrived in the east of Fife as ballast in the holds of Dutch merchant vessels and the style was later copied by local manufacturers. The house in the centre of the picture had an unusual curved forestair.

HYNE HEAD, BUCKHAVEN.

73166.J.V.

Hyne Head on a summer's day in 1909. The "L" shaped house on the right was "Hill Head House" and, like many of its neighbours it was built straight onto the rocks on the shore. This corner of the village was a particular favourite of the Victorian and Edwardian artists who came here in large numbers. The old man on the left is carrying a sma' line scull.

East End, Buckhaven, from Beach

The rocks in the foreground were known as the Hyne Rocks, formerly known as the "East Hyne". The range of rocks known as the "West Hyne" were incorporated into the West Pier of the 19th century harbour. It was these "hynes" or havens that gave the village its colloquial name "Buckhyne" which is still commonly used by local people.

This part of the village lay beyond the foot of East High Street. On the right of the picture was the coast road to Leven which was opened in 1895, but lasted for only eleven years. By 1960 the bing of the Wellesley towered above these houses and, not surprisingly they had been abandoned for the pollution was at its worst here.

The Links and Washer, Buckhaven

The hamlet of Links of Denbeath lay immediately to the east of Buckhaven, on the landward side of the coast road to Leven. The people of Buckhaven chose the Links as the site of their first church in 1794 and their first school in 1810. In 1905 the Wemyss Coal Company took over the lease of the Wellesley Colliery and in order to expand the workings there they urgently needed adjacent land to dump the waste from the mine. The Links lay on this land and Randolph Wemyss approached the Town Council for permission the buy the village and close the road. Permission was granted on the condition that a replacement road was constructed at no expense to the burgh. This was agreed and in 1906 Wellesley Road was opened from Muiredge to Aberhill.

The Links, Buckhaven

The evacuation of Links of Denbeath began in 1906 and the displaced families were rehoused in new buildings on College Street. This picture was taken during the last days of the Links. On the right a pair of houses have been fenced off and the bing has spilled over into what was once a garden. In the next block the end house has been boarded up and other boards are propped in readiness against its neighbours. The Links eventually disappeared completely under millions of tons of pit redd where it stays to this day, waiting like Pompeii for some future archaeologist.

The Washer, Denbeath

The Denbeath Pit was sunk in 1875 by Messrs. Bowman & Company under license from the landowner, the Laird of Wemyss. In 1905 Bowman's lease expired and the pit was taken over by the Wemyss Coal Company. A new shaft was opened and the mine was renamed the Wellesley Colliery. In 1906 the huge Baum coal washer was installed, dominating the local skyline. In 1947 1600 men were employed here and output exceeded 3,500 tons per day. The economy of the area took a staggering blow when the Wellesley closed in 1967. Sadly, despite the benefits it had undoubtedly brought to Buckhaven and its neighbours, the Wellesley Colliery was also responsible for perhaps the worst case of coastal destruction anywhere in Scotland. In 1972 the site was taken over by an oil rig construction firm and the bing was partly levelled.

A 1900 view taken from midway down East High Street, looking towards the shore. Today high flats on either side of this street have turned it into a gloomy cavern.

East High Street, Buckhaven.

The top of East High Street in 1905, with Gordon's Randolph Hotel on the right. The carriage outside was a horse-bus run by the proprietor.The two houses opposite the hotel were demolished in 1926 to make way for an extension to Buckhaven School. This building is the only one remaining to locate this scene.

College Street, Buckhaven.

The building on the right was opened in 1891 as the Town Hall of the newly created Police Burgh of Buckhaven, Methil and Innerleven. It served as the seat of local administration until the council was amalgamated into Kirkcaldy District Council in the 1970s. Sadly, many records were disposed of at this time and valuable historical information lost. Today the former town hall is a public library which also houses an interesting local museum.

College Street, Buckhaven.

Newly built houses in College Street in 1908. The street originally stopped at the junction in the middle distance of the photograph but was extended to link up with Wellesley Road in 1906.

HIGHER GRADE SCHOOL, BUCKHAVEN

Buckhaven's first public school was a subscription school, opened in 1862. It had only two classrooms, each with sixty pupils with a leaving age of twelve. Each scholar had to supply their own ink and some coal to heat the school! It was a so-called "Madras School", as students were entitled to apply for scholarships to continue their education at Madras College in St. Andrews. A two storey extension was added in 1892, and three years later Buckhaven School had the honour of becoming the first Higher Grade Public School in Scotland. In 1908 the old single storey building was demolished and replaced with a state-of-the-art modern building which took only four months to complete. This contemporary photograph shows the 1892 extension facing Church Street with the new school behind.

Buckhaven Higher Grade was a progressive establishment and recognised the need for vocational education to serve the needs of the industry that would ultimately employ many of its pupils. A four year course in mining was instituted, comprising classes in mining and geology, mathematics, chemistry, mine surveying, mine drawing and electricity. A mining school extension was added in 1926. In 1933 the school was renamed Buckhaven High. The present Buckhaven High School opened in 1957 and the old School was renamed Braehead Secondary. It was closed and demolished in 1971. Only the mining school extension remains and is now an annexe of the local technical college. The site of Braehead is now a landscaped garden.

Randolph street dates from around 1900 and was named after Randolph Wemyss. On the left of this 1904 picture are the new premises of Buckhaven Co-operative Society, which had been trading since 1868. So successful was the business that this short lived building was rebuilt and enlarged in 1909.

Buckhaven Co-op was the Edwardian ultimate in one-stop shopping, eventually boasting seventeen departments as well as nurseries at Buckhaven and Ladybank. In 1947 the society had over five thousand members. In the post war years improved bus services and increasing car ownership removed the need for many people to shop locally. Leven and Kirkcaldy increased in popularity and Buckhaven Co-op ran into financial difficulties. It merged first with the Sinclairtown Co-op, eventually being absorbed in the 1970s by the national "Co-op" chain. Local stores like Buckhaven were "rationalised" and by the mid 1980s only the grocery department was still trading. Today the whole building is boarded up and faces a doubtful future.

LAWRENCE STREET, BUCKHAVEN

The brick building on the right of this 1902 picture has been demolished, but otherwise there are few changes.

BURNS AVENUE, BUCKHAVEN.

96724.JV.

In 1919 Lloyd-George's coalition government passed the Scottish Housing Act following his election campaign promise of "homes fit for heroes". This act provided for the provision of new schemes of building, partly funded by Government and partly by local authority rates, to re-house workers living in sub-standard property. The first council houses at Buckhaven were begun in 1920 and within two years 186 homes had been completed. Each house had running water, a bathroom and gas cooker – sheer luxury to many of their first tenants. Although criticised at the time for their plain and repetitive appearance, these houses were convenient and modern. Regrettably, subsequent council architects have failed to equal their appeal.

WELLESLEY ROAD, BUCKHAVEN

The Wemyss and District Tramway car looks out of date alongside the new houses in this 1922 postcard. The tramway was started in 1906 by Randolph Wemyss, and ran between Scoonie Road, Leven and Rosslyn Street in Gallatown where it linked with the Kirkcaldy Corporation Tramway. In the 1920s competition from an increasing number of local motor bus operators pushed the tramway out of business, leading to its eventual closure in 1932.

Muiredge Pit, Buckhaven

In 1864 Archibald Bowman, and brothers James and David Cairns, bought the lease of Muiredge Colliery from the Wemyss Coal Company. The W.C.C. had sunk a shaft at Muiredge, but had struck burnt coal at a depth of 80 feet and considered the pit to have no potential. The three partners persevered with what seems to have been a speculative venture and were rewarded with the discovery that through the burnt layer lay an abundance of fine coal 100 feet down. In the early 1870s Messrs. Bowman & Co. capitalised on their success by opening three more collieries in the area; the Denbeath, the Isabella, and the Rosie. When David Cairns, the last of the three founders died in 1905, the leases of all the Bowman & Co. pits reverted to the Wemyss Coal Company. Muiredge was closed in 1928. In 1936 the old wooden pithead was demolished and a new seam opened with a steel replacement. Eventually, Muiredge became no more than an escape shaft from the Wellesley Colliery and was finally demolished in 1969.

Slaughter-house, Buckhaven.

Hardly a postcard which invites the message "wish you were here", but when Buckhaven's new abattoir opened at Muiredge in 1910 it was the latest in hygienic amenities. Having said that, this card didn't appear to have sold well, since I have only ever seen one copy!

Buckhaven Boy Scout Troup in 1911.